A Tree Bows Humbly With Fruit

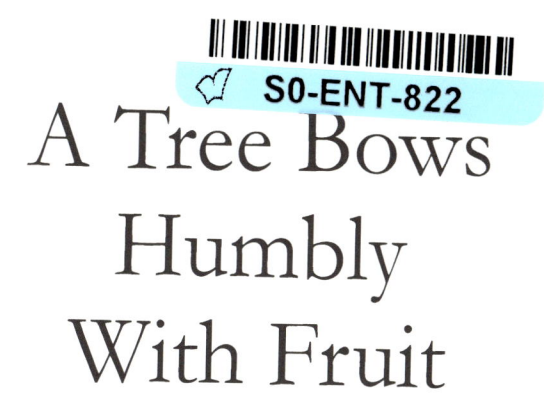

Poems

Józef Tracz-Ripple

Copyright © 2016 Józef Tracz-Ripple
& Multiverse Books

Front Cover Art: 17th Century depiction, Tree of Life, Palace of Shaki Khans, Azerbaijan; Azerbaijan National Art Museum, Usta Gambar Garabagi Copyright © 2016

All rights reserved.

ISBN: 1530373468
ISBN-13: 9781530373468

Józef Tracz-Ripple

Still, infinite droplet of Love:
moisture & vibration eternal.

Seed-maker.

CONTENTS

Acknowledgments

I: Plum-stones

II: Hollow Husks

III: Hush'd Hymns

IV: Harp Sounds

BLATHERING

none of these poems were written. they were not imagined in the brain's skewed imagination —what is called the "illusion of reality." these poems are breath: the wind through the reed, the aeolian harp's song, a tree's sigh of relief at the closed-eyed sight of the Silent One. they are neither the songs nor sounds of Love; they are its soft, nurturing vibration. there is more Mystery in the quivering of the violin string's longing than the sound they make. the song is our heart's love. the ripples in the water from the Friend's footsteps pressed into the earth is fountainhead Love. we are all nero playing our sad song while our city burns. Love is closest then. i've never written anything. i've never been anything. all i am is a shell enclosing eternal Love, cracking slightly for this Light to peer into open hearts.

"Even in the case of lifeless things that make sounds, such as the flute or harp, how will anyone know what tune is being played unless there is a distinction in the notes?" -(*Corinthians 14:7*)

φ

"Even the junipers and the cedars of Lebanon gloat over you and say, "Now that you have been laid low, no one comes to cut us down." -(*Isaiah 14:8*)

φ

"You saw a fire, and light came.
You saw blood, and wine
is being poured.

Don't run from your own tremendous good fortune.

Be silent and don't try
to add up what's been given.

An uncountable grace has come to you."
- Rumi

PLUM-STONES

φ

there've been so
many *ifs* in my life,
my basket would
nearly
over
      f
        l
          o
            w

but i,
in being clever,
drilled through the bottom, to let them all go.
and if there's anything
to ever teach or learn,
let it be this that i bestow:
love is never some thing you owe.
so be wise
in the dispersion
and placement of your seeds,
for, you cannot unreap what you sow.

ϙ

you are an empire
of love
and compassion.
share the wealth
of your loving-self
to all those
in dire need.

ϙ

date palm seeds
can go dormant
for decades
until the light
and water
conditions
are just right.

this is where
my love
has been,
waiting
for You.

φ

i dare you to get lost
in love's labyrinth.
there are no walls here.

only beauty
and the wild kiss
of confusion.

you will never have any thoughts
of leaving such comfort.

φ

i love my old friend,
the wind.

everything she touches
dances like drunkards.

this is the only way
i know how
to love you.

and you,
to love me.

φ

how many tears are required
to make the rain?

oh, look!

i've made the clouds

sad again

with my poems.

φ

how many mornings
have you lain awake
with tear-filled eyes

only wanting music,
yet you were annoyed
by the songs of birds?

we are all happy as hypocrites.

we are all crippled intellects.

teach your mind awareness of this.

φ

i've been drinking galaxies again,
while playing chess with you,
my beloved, my watchmaker.
the table has been tipped
too many times in my mad love
for the piece's movement.
when the stars are singing,
rest your lovely head here.

φ

i am a fool.

i take it back.

i desire nothing.

crush me into death.

give everything

to everyone

i love.

φ

i carry with me

only wicker hearts

and blooming fledglings.

be mad with longing

and reckless as fuck.

let your ego cart go

careening over

the cliff face.

you no longer need its baggage.

burn your bones to ash

and fill my sky with blood.

throw away your Life vest.

plunge soul-first
into the river
of Love.

φ

when we are both

in silent communion,

i see gold waves vibrate

like rays of sunlight

streaking across a beautiful

evening summer sky.

φ

consciousness:

a chemical process.

"I want": a reflex.

who is the i, or what?

reflections on the river,

easily rippled away.

there is a division

i cannot speak.

but i can touch it.

all this fading and dying.

only words, no reality.

two birds making love

in the bushes are more

valuable than one

trapped within a hand.

that is freedom.

not these thoughts,

nor the containing cage.

silence
your
every
atom,

until you are just

a breathing star.

φ

how many trees

have you put your

lips to in the Silent Kiss?

not nearly enough,

i assure you.

get completely drunk

in the meadow of gold,

where all flower stems

grow mystical gems!

inside me, i heard

your mouth open to smile.

i'm lost.

there aren't enough thorns

in all the worlds

to deter me

from your Rosy Love.

φ

your name etched into me

with blades made for stone.

i am grateful for permanence

in a world of impermanence.

φ

Al-Khafid: الخَافِض

ego
raises
its voice.

Your blade takes
trophy tongues.

Your hands make
manna from teeth
crushed to powder.

ego stares back
in anger with
malice black eyes.

You pluck the orbs
and they become earths
in different worlds.

Still. it swings fists, undying.

With a Kiss,
You break the bones
that let it stand.

it lies limp, moaning.

i bleed from everywhere.

i am crying, "Thank You!"

***

Within the Palace of Silence,
 you will find...

This is where Love lives.

φ

Once,

my pride was large.

my heart was small.

i was so ignorant.

i thought i knew it all.

φ

Your straw broke my camel's back.
Your needle hid perfectly in my haystack.

People lost in thought or words,
or
thoughtless
words.

i hid
in Your
pomegranate garden,

just
waiting for the sight of You.

φ

let me be the grass rising up
to be trampled by the Giant's Foot!

i've been singing to a bird in my chest-chimney,
and now i'm covered in all your Love soot!

i've been having recurring flying dreams.
and i'm at your bedside, again, while you talk, asleep.
Your words become my days that come and go.
Your words become rain where hyacinth grow.

φ

Know this now:

Every single moment, right now,

is golden fruit that has been

placed in your basket, without

cause or want of return. taste

that fruit and allow your heart's

strings to tune up with the rest

of this beautiful universe band.

Do what your heart whispers to you.

Follow the pull of Love

and nothing else.

φ

Selfishness is your only source of sadness.
Let it go.
Let it flutter away into the night,
with broken wings.
change your address,
so it cannot find you again.

Keep a close
watch on my heart,
my dear Friend.

my eyes are tired and blind.

i want that selflessness
that will melt mountains
back into the sea,

that will return river
rain to the sky,

that will return fruit seeds
to the earth,

that will return stars back
into the night Womb.

All the Love that will
return me back to You.

φ

in every soundless poem

that i paint of you, i keep

your eyes closed, because

they are a secret that only

You and i get to keep.

φ

Can you feel the energy

when the Sun is touching you?

Can you feel the entropy

when Love is dissolving you?

φ

And why would i want anything

from this whole world?

Everything can only be a

memory i hold until i die.

How many times have you been

shamed out of misplaced fear,

too afraid to see your own

creation looking from the mirror?

φ

In the woods at night, i walk
with an unlit candle in hand.

You speak through the owl mouth
above me, asking "Hu?"

it is I, yusuf, it is You!
it is your other face!
it is your sunshine smile!

i'm searching in the dark
for your snares and traps.

quiet now. i hear laughter in silence.

my candle becomes a burning bush.

we have a friend down there!

i lower my rope and pull hard.

a basket of flowers rises up
and covers me.

suddenly,
it is daylight.

i can never be a pronoun.

unless You're in there,

pulling all the mad gears.

φ

Today, i started giving back

for all i've been given.

Yes, i've been selling back

some things that were loaned to me.

The time will be coming

when the complete exchange

of return is due, so i continue

to lend back pieces over time,

where i am slowly dissipating

back into mother nature.

Her exhale will one day

be inhaled,

and i shall go with it

φ

Friend, you hold me

in warm hands.

again, i am dead.

but You are life-bringer.

my bird heart fluttered

too madly from your Love.

i've flown into the window

just trying to touch You.

but this body is a prison,

where you sit inside,

and we are lovers

separated by the glass

only able to talk with minds.

Voice has never been so obsolete.

Love so inexplicable.

φ

What is fame and recognition?
—people hearing

What is Love?
—God listening

φ

in the Great Love,
i am rising in confusion.
bewildered like smoke,
i come from flame
and quickly disintegrate
my uncontainable form
back into the wind.

a knock at my door.

it is Truth, in beggar garbs,
delightfully wanting only my attention.

"I've been looking for You —
but You found me instead!"

My Friend steps through
the doorway,
and everything
in the room is forever Light.

φ

i've lived the life of body,

draped in the veil of pleasure:

sea flooding sea.

then the life of mind:

self-pleasure of *knowledge*.

Then the life of soul:

endless-particle-waves,

connectivity and connection.

Finally: a new realm, unexplainable.

"Who are you and where did you
come from?" She asked me.

Now,
i do not know answers
to either of these questions.

HOLLOW HUSKS

Knock it off.
Quit trying so hard.
It's all coming.

φ

i don't know if You exist.
i hardly know if i do.

i feel something…indefinable.

all of my incapabilities
of explanation or understanding.

even if You are not you.
the message, the purpose,
the point
are all the same to me:

Be kind, be aware.
Give love, give compassion,
endlessly until you die.

φ

Everything was false.

A presentation to the senses.
Nothing more than that.

Now i see beyond seeing.
My eye's Light cut through.

My soul is both fruit and sweetness.

i do not love you.

Instead, i want to fall in love
with learning how
we must all Love one another.

φ

An event, a happening, a thing.

In original essence, a purity.

Anything that stems from this

original source is distortion,

creation, and illusion.

Our words and ideas we apply
like a bandaid
to an imagined wound.

We build around us detachment
and disconnect from the Source.

These thoughts are unavoidable.

But acknowledge, then let go.

Pass no judgement on anything.
Simply let it all be, and rejoice
in the beautiful fact of your life,
and that anything happens at all.

And if you're bored, my god,
you are not boring.
You just haven't
opened your goddamned eyes yet

to take
a real
good look
around.

φ

i don't know how it all happened.
but i stood facing two wolves,
one black and one white.

the symbolism was irrelevant.

rabid-faced, teeth hung on display
as they locked eyes with each other.

Past and future, all duality,
seeing into the mirror, inverted.

i felt the fissure tear through
my ego, dividing self and unself.
like an earthquake, but there was
only silence rather than vibration.

i stood outside of them both,
just watching the futility feud.

i cut the ropes and the curtain fell.

Hurled back into nothingness,
i heaved my sentient library,
all the stained and frilled pages
filled with words that never
really meant anything to anyone.

How often have you cowered
at your unguarded self?

How many times have you turned
the eye inward to see it looking back?

Is there any answer, any reply to the
capital Mystery with a question?

i can no longer differentiate the reply.

These, and all ideas, i am no longer
here for.

i pick up a stone
from the sand,
raise it to my lips,
then toss
it into the water,
just to rid myself
of the separation,
just to hear the
sound of laughter,

because i refuse
to open my true mouth
for anyone who isn't you.

ϙ

i was present when you painted the world,
and with each new color you picked up,
i jumped for joy!

When you let the trees grow their own
way and you gave us limbs to move.

Perhaps, the path to a gentle soul
is not always the most gentle one.

All this water and i can't even begin
to wonder where it all came from –
or even more, how it all stays?

It takes boiling and burning
to remove most impurities.

There are only two things i can say
that i know:

one is confusion.
the other is i don't know.

φ

A regal moth had holes in her wings,
yet she still flew so beautifully.

There are mysteries that defy reason.
Give your life to become one of them.

φ

i long to be your equal, simply
to be as a true friend to you,
where mutual appreciation lives.

In love, let us be nothing more
than homebuilders on this earth.

i'll quiet every molecule and
element contained within me,
when i watch your lips begin to move.

ϕ

Faith may move mountains,
but only Love will climb them.

the Friend's shadow may sleep
in seeds underneath all,
but atop, you can begin to
taste the scent of Her lips.

The way may be carved by
feet or by heart.

There is no telling which is which.

There is no tegument or fig leaf.
Only the opening abides.

The lamb removed the gates,
and the lion came kissing my wounds.

An author must
sever the head
from the body
and be like a candle,
burning still
continuously
from
the flame
stuck in their wax.

ϕ

Can you imagine a world without meaning?

Birds would not have wings.
Trees would not have leaves.
Rivers would never flow.
There would be no ocean.
Hearts would fall into disuse
through years of evolution.
Mind would be reduced
to a broken tape recorder.

everything just burning up
and melting in the absence
of the sun's passionate love.

φ

Every thought: a pebble or mala bead
inside my mind, counted and recounted.
Every non-thought, the disappearance
of stones, the atom's unfurling.

Is there a middle ground?

A bird dissolves into the air
as i look upward at the sky.

There is only one mind, not my own.

i am sifting through dark matter
searching for a hidden doorway.

This world is entirely a projection:

my inward mind, reaching outward,
longing for the sight of Breath.

But where am i
to locate
the True Eye?

That telescope
that peers lovingly at All?

φ

Suspension of disbelief
and cognitive estrangement
are a bridge with no ground –
yet the Heart walks along
perfectly fine and untouched.

What do you want or
do you not even know?

Heart never longs for material things.
only the Other Heart that is both
without and beyond materiality.

φ

Churches make for good kindling
and religions for oxygen and fuel.

Alright, take it easy.
They're just words.

Don't forget that you burn inside
a sacred heart that also burns inside you,
where neither walls nor rules hide.

φ

My eyes here
are as
worthless
as gold stones.

Give me new sight,
please,

or take
this one away.

φ

There is not one moment
where my thoughts do not hold you.

My mind is the calm sea
murmuring soundless secrets.

You sit in lotus pose
atop my third eye,
smiling at my true self.

Naked and shameless,
contained and freed with your Love,
i am dancing like a reed in the wind,

waiting to become your food,

or your music,

or your words.

φ

Little Angels sit in the same
room that i do. They're hearts
are so powerful i am disarmed
and overwhelmed by them.
Such dark hair and dark eyes,
and such tiny collar bones.

These beautiful miniature princesses.
How much i wish to kiss you,
and your mother and father,
and then i realize that you are
all already dancing inside me.

Such beauty, too humble to
draw attention to itself everywhere.

φ

God may be silent.

But there is always

a finger that is

pointing everywhere!

φ

What a quandary?
How wyrd?

You smile into the mirror.
And it smiles back.

φ

The big bad wolf sits outside
the door of the three little pigs.

Inside, they are shaking with fear.
Outside, wolf is crying with separation.

φ

Relax!
Laugh!
All of you!

God has a tremendous
sense of humor.
After all,
who created it in the first place?

φ

i want nothing!

how am i to know

what i truly want?

i am cold, you give warmth.

too hot! you give cold, i freeze.

How to calm the sea tempest?

φ

Lovers say, "Where have you been
all of my life?" but really what is
being spoken is this: "How did i
never notice you inside of me
all of this time!?" Then, thinking:
"I'm sorry it took me so long to
find myself, because in doing
so, it seems i have found you."

φ

Let Love's crowbar

tear the soul shell

off of your bones.

Let that beautiful

Friend come dancing

out into your inner Light

like a drunk donkey

too in Love to stand.

φ

The blind storyteller

blathers inside us all.

Why do we keep

buying him drinks?

He knows nothing of truth.

He has no vision.

So why do we listen,

even when our

ears are magmic?

Why do we keep eating lava,

when the fruit is hanging,

eager to be consumed?

The Silent One sits

in the shade of the Heart Tree,

waving and gazing at you

with Her perfect Love Eyes.

φ

The journey is inward.
The absence of movement.

Yet. Still movement.
Infinite mobility.

We shift and transform
at a single point in spacetime.

Yet. Soaring through
every particle in existence…
touching everything…

being everything and
nothing all at once.

φ

The Door is open.
fear wants it closed.
Release that from Heart.

Feel the Sun set on your fur.
Roll around in Love
with no expectations.

  don't want what i want.
  nly what will be.

φ

Is it just a mockingbird trying

to imitate Your Voice?

What is sound anyways?

Is this water or fire?

Am i drowning or burning?

Is there even a difference?

The mountains are inside my soul,

crying, and i can't find them to

comfort with gentle hands.

i am a worthless bat soaring,

and Thunder is everywhere.

A complete mindfuck of

total disorientation to everything.

φ

My emptiness is clawing at the Door,
wanting wanting more, Your Fullness.
Death is my only earthly love.

i've wrapped too many cobwebs
of ugliness around all Your Beauty.

Human, all too human — shameful.

Too many half loves.

A glass half full is still empty!

i squeeze it in my hand,
until i can feel the glass implode
inside of my grasp and the pieces

in my hand. Not nearly enough
blood to even begin to offer You.

Give me the Circling Light i see
everywhere!...

...but cannot touch.

φ

Regaining sight through the Heart.
Do you hear this thunder
that i am making for you?

Do my wings or chest beat faster?

fear is chained to the earth.
i've left it behind now.

if it is your death that awaits me,
then i will take the blessing.

i know the inextinguishable.

i welcome the water to the other fire.

ϕ

The hypocrites scream words

of nonresistance in the face of war!

But when Love shows up,

they become armed to the teeth!

ϕ

A blackbird had scars on his wings,
which brought terrible pain to open
them at all, but love was all that
filled his bird heart, and he loved
the little bird, so he chased her
everywhere she soared, through
the entire sky. He circled the sun
to warm his lips to kiss her
when she got cold, and he
laid infinite roses at her feet.

φ

i have nothing to give or offer
to you, my dearest love, other
than this temporary body
that will surely perish.

All i can ever do is point
towards the light around
and within you and kiss
that soft spot on your chest,

where Greatness sits awake

within your Golden Heart.

φ

Don't forget that when the sand is
being thrown in your eyes and your
teeth are being kicked in, that all of
the beauty is still around you. So don't

swing fists in the dark. Lay down. It's
okay if you cry a little. The Love is
coming to snuggle your sad bones
and kick your mind off the cliff since

you've been thinking too much about
nothing. The Love is here, always.
And it's so happy to kiss your face.

It brought Light to everything.

ϕ

i double-lovedog dare you

to eradicate this smile from my face.

There is too fucking much love

to contain within a single fixed place.

i can barely stand, but fuck this body.

It is nothing compared to your grace.

i was made by hands a specific way.

The only one able to consume your flame.

φ

Sometimes, i am a bee.
So i can feel the flower's hug.

Sometimes, i am the ground.
So i can feel your touch all the time.

Sometimes, i am the dirt.
So i can feel you growing out of me.

Sometimes, i am a butterfly.
So i can dance with the air.

Sometimes, i am the cloud.
So i can hold all your tears.

Sometimes, i am the moon.
So i can pet the sleeping sun's hair.

Sometimes, i am a lover.
So i can know the Beloved.

Sometimes, i am a friend.
So i can be your friend.

Sometimes, i am a book.
So you can read my burning soul.

Sometimes, i am a grape.
So i can make you feel drunk.

Sometimes, i am food.
So you are never hungry.

Sometimes, i am a star.
So i can brighten your dark spots.

Sometimes, i am tickle in your lung.
So you remember to laugh.

Sometimes, i am music.
So you can hear beauty call.

All the time, i am everything for you.
All the time, i am always here for you.

φ

These tears, so selfish and sad.

Yet, gentle reminders of the Love.

Kid memories of tasting the ocean
in all Her majestic vastness. Pouring
from inside something as small as me.

Were you there holding my hand?

Or have i imagined my entire life?

φ

i can no longer tell:

am i falling apart
or have i never been
put together, and i am
falling into shapelessness?

Such confusion arises
as i try to "build"
amongst all this disintegration.

Yet, nothing matters.

There is no more need for thoughts.

i must simply find a way back to You.

φ

Who has salted my earth?

Who has broken my eyes,
my mouth, my lungs?

How do we let go of what
we feel we never really held?

How do i kiss the Friend?

Or does even that hold secret motives?

How do i comfort my brother,
when my own corpse is filled
with flaming arrows of great loss?

Rumi sends out looking for Shams.

How does even god's friend
have a heart that limps?

All i can ever feel is Love.
Even though it obliterates me.

Just shake me out of your shoes
like the meaningless sand i am.

φ

There is a secret hidden within

the bellowing laugh of the Dalai Lama.

It comes from inside of him,

yet it is pulled from a different

dimension. And i hear this sound

as i sit across from him, pointing

towards the mountain outside his

window, while i lift the hacksaw to

myself and start talking frantically

about birds, specifically vultures.

In a dream, you held my hand.
In a dream, you kissed my sad face.
In a dream, you freed me from it.

But dreams are reality and reality
 is but a dream and this incomprehensible
madness just continues twirling to
the Mystery in circles, like Rumi's
sadness, ad infinitum,

and i am your loneliness at the Center.

φ

The true gift of a face is that
it can never hide the true self.
So if you took a closer look,
you'd see how many ruins
are inside of me, where the
winds rush insane and wild,
where i am trying desperately
to pitch my tent in your Heart.

φ

i would sing when i knew you

were coming to me.

But my only memory is of you

leaving on that day.

The soft plums falling hard

against the fresh spring earth.

φ

But if all this crying

does not end in laughter,

then we are all seriously

doing something wrong.

φ

This living is not easy,
even with all Your Beauty.

But the difficulties are love.
And the death is reward.

It seems the brighter you burn,
the more you burn yourself.

But that's okay too.

Just look at all the perfect stars.

Even they are all collapsing
inwards and imploding,
burning themselves alive.

It is a great comfort
to feel exactly like them.

φ

This great pain is made of beauty.

A wrecking ball hitting the center

of the house that was built.

An opening. A huge doorway.

It must be big enough.

It is where the Friend enters,

where She comes with Love.

To heal. To mold you into Light.

φ

One of my favorite stories
has always been the Tale
of the Two Wolves.
It is beautiful, but incomplete to me.

It forgets a really important detail:
How to tell which wolf is which?

Simple: starve them both.

fear will growl and bite you. But
Love will sit by your side and kiss you.

φ

i thought that i had broken,
then a hand took mine, and
it led me through the desolate
city of all my sorrows and ruins.

A Face i've always known, a Brother.

In robes of Light, holding my
hand, we are laughing and
singing songs to all of our Loves.

φ

This language of confusion!

It is no coincidence with these things:

Silence is universal!

Smiling is universal!

Laughing is universal!

Love is universal!

These all speak enough.

φ

i prayed for a friend.
And the Friend came.

i cried all alone.
And i felt You hold me.

i prayed for rain.
And i watched it start to Rain.

i prayed for an opening.
And you pulled the string
that made my skeleton stand.

φ

You think of my hand lifting,
and i watch it lift.

In your name, only silence.

Angel's with fingers entwined.
Like them, we are honeysuckle vine.
No more you and i.

A complex enigmatic puzzle buried
within this confusing labyrinth.

How many broken teeth will fall out
and become plants in the earth?

How much beauty can pour from
a single mouth, a single wound?

i reach out my arms to hug You,
but i am way too small,

so i just hug Myself.

φ

i am a star, broken
inside and burning.
eating nothing but air,
waiting for the end of madness.

ϙ

Dilemmas, dilemmas:
What do i wear today?
What should i eat?
What am i going to do later?

i myself am more focused:
How do i unbreak?
How do i heal others?
How do i place more love
in this world before i am gone?

ϙ

This is a metaphor for the absence
of metaphors. No more. Never again.

i am light years away.
i am a song like your beautiful face.

Here, i am so distant and far,
walking in the shadow of a friend.
How spooky i've become.

i walk from billions of miles away,
like a ghost, slipping directly
into your delicate, open heart,

my hands filled with Light.

φ

What am i doing?

Where am i going?

Complete nonsense to me.

All i can do is say gently:

"Lead me to You."

If you like me,

perhaps i'll find a friend

along this way.

i'm tired of covering myself

in my own wolf's blood.

i'm sleepy at the thought

of being a silly sheep.

φ

i shut my eyes and calm my breath
to slow down the world around

and focus on the sound surrounding.
In the distance to the left ridge,

upon high, soft and heavy paws
pressing ferns into soft grounds.
Have you come for my death,

or have i come for yours?

High above us both, the songbird
chirps a plea for Love against

the sky, and i open my Heart's doors,
so you can walk freely inside.

φ

This is the pattern lovers make,
when their minds are too tired
from thinking, when the heart
can stretch its wings outward
to fully encompass the other.

This is the pattern lovers make,
when their lips are too tired
from all the kissing, and worse,
the talking, which is only
a hobbling drunk of true feeling.

This is the pattern lovers make,
when their souls finally kiss,
and they become the Source
of all that will ever exist.

φ

How many drunken circles
can i walk in the woods tonight?

Can you hear my silence?

i am your atoms and your blood.

i am the galaxies stacked inside
and in that entangled dancing overhead.

It is not a choice or will:

my love made to orbit you.

φ

A pileated woodpecker taps

the sketch of my heart sounds

into a tree nearby over the stream.

i put my lips on the fern,

and i watch its leaves stretch

outwards as two white butterflies

flap their wings out from underneath,

making love in the air they breathe.

φ

do you really need to be
beaten with a rainbow
for your mind to let go
and see the loving beauty
in all the storms?
perspective.
i do not know yours.
but i am learning, gratefully.
a single pixel.
a single atom.
within my eye holds the entire universe.
and it itself is a universe within a universe.
inwards and outwards,
all is contained.

i sit perched in your palm
like a songbird, and i have so many
more songs to sing to you.

i am only beginning.

and yet, somehow...the mystery...
within the eye's atom,
the palm
that holds the songbird
is also inside me there,

and inside of my heart.
what a perfect circle you've created.

love grows in a circle.
it appears as an orb.

φ

i see the pattern.
all of your angels are weeping.
am i one of them?
we are not crying over loss.
we are not crying out of pain.
we are crying at what is coming.
we are crying cause your face is near.
the image has always been blurred.
but tear-eyed, it reassembles for us.

the giant's heart is rising from the bottom of the ocean.

φ

the heart is a golden ratio.

the soul is a loxodrome.

Love loves circles,

guiding you always to Her.

you feel you're chasing your tail,

but that is divine progress,

to move in such beautiful motion.

there are telescopes that peer

far into the dark night above.

and there are invisible telescopes

that peer deeply inward

to find Love, the unnameable

constellation maker.

φ

Everyone is getting drunk
shooting their arrows at each other,
hoping they'll hit their mark.

Oh, those lovers with mad minds.

i send just one straight into the sky
with a prized feather tied to the tail.

You are a star. i watch it brush against
your skin, and the feather ignites.

i turn myself into nothing but a candle.

Everyone tries cutting my head off.

But then the arrow returns
and sticks in my neck.

i laugh as the wick catches fire.

φ

Cannibal Love.

Phototroph Heart.

Light-eater and Giver.

Is it wave or particle,

or is it the Unseen?

A drunk derivative is lost

in the Formula's crowd.

Where does this infinity symbol

disjoint its spine to curl

backwards from and to You

like circles forever encircling?

The dragon is eating Her tail again.

The oculus points upwards at orbits.

i guess all rivers run together.

φ

My longing is the hummingbird,
soaring wings and the infinite.

You promised no more rain,
no more flooding this world.
But i crave those willow tears.

i cut my wrists and watch
the blood geysers rush into the sky!

Send the birds from your boat!

All the rainbows come out to do
backbends around your Heart.

φ

For how long have i dreamt of Egypt?
the eleven stars, the twining sun and moon?
the grapes were being pressed.

all the terra cotta kisses upon my face.
we were inseparable: Abram's turtledove.
inside me, for only you, are stars and rivers.

i carry a burning lamp, walking into your heart.
like a leaf too in love to ever be contained,
i've found my way, spiraling back into You.

HUSHED HYMNS

this is a nice little dance
our egos have been doing.
but my heart is tired from it.
i want that real soul stuff.

φ

become anything but what you think you are.

if you could sit atop trees just to see,
perhaps you would laugh like the crow does.

if you could weave webs through the night,
perhaps you would imitate stars and
do the spider's circling love dance.

i know it is very hard, but please,

become anything but what you think you are.

φ

i have already spoken too much,
so let me say not another word

for what is to come.

are you nothing?

let what speaks to your core
speak for you.

there are grapes of silence,
drink from them with a closed mouth.

this wine of the infinite will make you limitless.

how many songs have died in your heart today?

i am but one.

φ

[only fragments of these works remain]

φ

and in this connection to something,
has it all come from nothing?
but what hides in this illusion
other than the nonexistence of division?

you can see me everywhere.
but you'll never hold me.
like light theories, i do not exist.

i am somewhere beyond names,
meaning, duality, philosophies.

neither something nor nothingness,
not even between, just a connecting.
from this world and another.
from the seen and the unseen.

φ

is this competitive realty,
this inner space?
how many rooms are available?
how many thoughts, cells, pores,
synapses, or embryonic light?
i am sweeping all of the dust
from the hardwood floors.
a tough cleaning and polishing
to see the shadow reflect back.
so many skies and moons
inside of my heart and lungs.
so much of my heart and lungs
inside the starlight and stardark.

φ

you must learn the laughter
of my Friend and i.
my love will easily take flight
like a crow in the dead of night.
my Friend is all that is light,
and when i run alongside Her,
we both immediately vanish.

there is magic in how
you mix two colors together
and create one anew.

there is mystery in how
two lovers fall together
to perform the invisible act.

φ

i am making a mother of the motherless.
i snap my fingers
and all the zoo fences
and cages vanish,
so your wild animal
heart will roam free.

i am making day out of night
and a sea out of sand.
ive planted rows of roses
underneath your ribs
before you were even born.

i am making a father out of nothing.

ive built you
a sailing vessel
before rainbows
even formed in your eyes.

φ

i've spent too much of my life
not being as observant as i should,
to learn that wolves run with wolves,
to see the pale horse drinking from
my heart's pond with eagerness.
i've choked on marbles, or were they suns?

i will tell you that the burning
of the lover is not for everyone.

and that you and death are alike…

φ

not a player but a participant.

love that'll make a bird fall from the sky.

right now, i am exactly where
i need to be at exactly the right time.

there are no mistakes to be made.

if it must be, give me only pain.

wrap me in blankets of flame.

again, again change my heart's shape

φ

some: drowning
others: reaching for a raft
me: walking on water
this Love is soul craft.

φ

stop limiting yourself
with thinking
that is only contained
in this imaginary world.

stop building cages around yourself.
there is no such thing.

to some i appear as the invisible.
to others i may appear like smoke.

and yet to more, sometimes a friend
with a strong mouth that loves kissing you
and herculean ears that can not only hear you
light years away but can listen incessantly for eternities,
not to mention a heart that is comfortable enough to seat
one, if you are ever stranded on your path.

φ

with vision so small,
the heart is almost nonexistent.
so i willingly conspire with leeches,
hopeful that they taste my sweet blood
and it changes their sad soul.

φ

i will only ever let someone
love me who learns to love me from afar.

you can not see the meadow
by staring at a single flower.

i, in seeing you with love,
see you as both flower
and field all contained.

and when we are finally close,
there is a closing of the eyes
and mouth, eclipsed by the heart's opening.

it is only here,
where i can take your hand
and lie under and atop the sky.

φ

[i am in love with the queen of circles]

HARP SOUNDS

have you leapt into the heart of the volcano?
my blood is burning and will melt you down.
back to nothing. you want me to be nothing?
i am nothing. dont be afraid to be.

ϕ

do i unveil slowly
or should i tear
the rug out from
underneath your heart?

there are wounds we carry.
blood-dripped trails to our past.

and it is okay.

we are butchered and maimed
by the lure and the hook.
but step into the unseen i contain,
and i'll lick all the red drops away.

ϕ

i get way too drunk

and lie at mountains' feet.

waiting for avalanches

of butterflies.

too in love with possibility.

φ

the moon and i play cat and mouse,
and i flood gasoline into this shell house.
there's more love in a glowing circle
and a blowing silent angel's kiss.
quietude to the heart's solitude.
how long have i loved you —
since long before your birth?

φ

how much lost time spent searching
for love at the bottom of maelstroms?

how many of my hearts have i
thrown into the centers of quicksand?

beware the some who say friend
but in truth are a Mariana trench.

ive been obsessed with spinning.
ive been drunk with drowning.

your gentleness sings shyly upwards
through the coffer from rose lips:

your love-built pantheon inside me.

ϕ

"with dripping coconut lips:
in truth, it was only Love

that could make the shy

Moon's Face so filled with Light."

ϕ

i am hydrophobic
at the separation.
this craving for completion.

i am melting myself into the sun
to become a sunbeam,
to give you my warm touch
wherever you are.

such a heavy heart
sunken in the space net,

where all your light
playfully curls around me.

φ

don't ever accept an unworthy love
into your perfect little heart.
that coldness will paralyze
your butterfly wings.
but i have always been your sunrise,
awaiting the time-shift and star-twirl,
peeking my face over your heart horizon,
up above the mountain,
your light body,
flying in my sky.

φ

fall in love with a pathologist,
someone blind to form.

a doctor who studies the root
of your suffering in order to remove it.

someone who's mind only perceives
your insides and the beauty there.

do not focus on a face or fingers
or breasts or the knees and feet.

focus on the part that makes these
things instruments of love:

the place of laughter and kissing.
the tools for touching and holding.
the food source of new life.
a depiction on how to rise and stand.

the body is more often than not
just covered in changing cloth.

find the Lover of *faraji* inside:

the naked mad woman who

has torn all the robes off

and is dancing Light.

φ

our hearts are just diamonds
waiting to be unearthed
by the holy hands of our
own private archaeologist,
sent from the future
to find us and bring it to Light.

φ

close your eyes
until all you can
see is darkness.
wait in it and breathe deeply.

i left a trail of light there
for your heart to follow.

φ

i heard my heart
singing into the
mouth of a bird
from across the world.

φ

there is not reflex to possess.
i've melted the mind in love's fire.

fear of finality creates all illusion.
let it all go, the time has come.

you come floating like a flower
down the blood river into my heart.

wherever you want to be and must
is the only place i want for you.

φ

[do we dance for the stars or do they dance for us?]

i sat crying
and the tears
fell and formed
oceans on the earth.
in them, i saw the sky.

it was all a mirror now.

my other soul!
it is you!
i cried more.

my heart was free.

ϙ

there is no longer a józef.
i jumped into the heart of the volcano.
i dove head first into the blender.
i did a backflip off a star into the ocean's soul.

i no longer feel.
instead,
i have become Love.

ϙ

i stood underneath a heaven-tree,
contemplating the mystery,
and i suddenly felt moisture everywhere.

you leapt, bird-winged from above
and landed in my open palms,

so i held you and ran away laughing.

φ

i knew i recognized you,

the divine's Love bird.

all of the illuminated, shimmering

stardust throughout all space

is the painting on your wings.

all planets are atoms in your feathers.

you've spread for me, lifted me.

and now i need not ever read

another love story again,

because we've been writing

the greatest with our hearts.

φ

for how long have our souls been married?
since before the first star burst.

we sat watching that firework display.
we made love as the lights came on.

we were kissing as the orbs formed,
as the water came out of nothing,
nothing but Love,
as the trees began raising
their arms upwards in praise,
as the first song filled the
bird's trembling throat
and the clouds were crying
so happily from this feeling.

φ

how to find love:
{stab out your eyes.
become a friend of the friend in all hearts}

φ

drunk with separation

burning like the moon.

a cool white flame

to be a nightlight for you,

until your loving fingers

are here to hold my hand

and calm my heart in silence.

φ

go ahead and get heavier.

ripen.

your fruit is only getting sweeter

and the boughs are bending

to bring you closer

to the earth again.

♈

infinity is making love to infinity,

trying to find the mass of my heart.

my only ever Love, she is uncontainable

in every possible way.

she is a star stretched far in space.

she is the center in my homey heart place.

only god knows the words to speak

of my perfect little moonface.

♈

intellect is an illusion, a growing outwards as a parallax flower, our petal'd perspective. tumbling evolution. the endless serpent tackling its own tail, like a kitten in full play. how could you put money down on this table to bet, when there is no money or table? ah, but we are inters and all love the feeling of the hunt, even though we are the hunted.

φ

i reach my hand into the dark closet,

and i can feel my flesh tickle.

thousand year old laughter calls

and my soul begins rolling

through love's crazy grass

like a dog glowing in sunbeams.

how long have you been calling me?

my ears needed to be born.

when did i step into sleep

but slip inward to the invisible dream?

we danced touching faces

in that divine interior room of rooms.

then your gentle kiss sent me

flying like a dandelion

to my dearest darling's feet.

φ

we place our arrow
into the tense bow.
it pierces our own heart.

we throw the seeds
into the air as we run.
a meadow blooms inside.

we look through
Love's binoculars.
we see our Friend within.

you can turn the sun upside down
and he will still love you the same.
you can put my body in the ground,
my love will still sing your name.

φ

you put the bird's nest
in the ecstatic lover's heart.
the drunken singing was you
from within toward me.
centuries later, i return
the call like an echo.
but time and distance
are not what they first seem.
there is no end to a circle.
it is merely a curve, like
an eager finger on a globe.
or the lover's lips, silently
pressing onto their beloved.

φ

everyone points to god
in all the pretty things:
flowers there!
songbirds near!

this is obvious.
but Love is a heart
that dances everywhere.
the secret is closer
in an unknown way.

rest, then open your eyes at night.
She is hiding in your garden onions
growing wildly with the moon's light.
take a quick taste of Her.

your eyes are quickly truth's tears.

φ

birth is not a single event.
it is a continuous unfurling.
we take a knife to the world,
trying to cut it into pieces.
we sever ourselves, again again.

a watered seed in soil,
breaking a shell and growing.
the green stem reaching through dirt and shit,

it leaves darkness
and is struck down
with Love's eternal Light.

that's when Life truly begins.

a pink flower emerges
humbly as a mirror.
the petals wilt, clouds cry.

yet! a strawberry begins to form
giving you the taste of sweetness.
strawberry lips could only kiss the world.

god's loving perennial.
i come season after season,
ripe from the beloved's palm,
present to breathe the silent Light.

φ

the separation of our hearts
is looking with closed eyes.
we are solipsistic planets.
the orbs open like flowers
into the love and light.
i wiggle my grape lose
to fall into your earth touch.
i am heaved into the vat,
aging and dying alone,
crushed into this kind annihilation.
you drink me.
i taste freedom.

only through obliteration
do i learn that you
were the earth, roots,
and vines that always held me.

our lips were always figure eights.

so if you ever feel alone,
pluck a basil leaf and mash it
with your teeth: it is me.

φ

i have been too long embarrassed
by my meager cup, but realized
the wine is held the same by it.

similarly, i have been too long
ashamed of my nakedness,
but ive torn the robes
only to realize it was *pollution*
covering up all of the burning night stars.

now i am a fire in the love-atom
of every created thing.
i am no longer *a* thing
but a particle of *The* thing within all.

i see the sun's sacred heart
wearing the crown of light,
smiling through a bird's smile
during the orange dawn's call.

φ

i've flung scales and calculators
into the open burning volcano.

the heart within love is more precise.

it is golden and unquantifiable.

the ignorant when dead
are buried with their jewels.
but lovers are buried alive
like apeiron precious stones.

φ

humans begin by babbling
then speak the word "mine."
but birds begin babbling
then quickly sing into the sky.

standing upright,
we become forgetful
on how to bow.

trees lifting their limbs in Light-grace,
yet we continually cut them down.

i lean my head against the magnolia
and apologize for all we have done.

but i find laughter is the fuel
inside of the setting Love-burnt sun.

ϕ

if you don't believe
in the divine
or her dancing miracles,
look deep into
the flower's longing:
you will see how
an ecstatic beggar
from Konya
has had his prayer answered,
when his heart blossomed
inside of mine.

ϕ

foolishness:
looking toward the sky.

ignorance: a sledgehammer crushing
the pyramids into a fine dust.

misguided: pulling the sepulchre's stone away
or unearthing the dargah.

only emptiness resides there!
why are you there looking!?

i am all around you.

hidden.
like water and circles.

φ

it is known that we are clay.
see the invisible pinhole, where
the divine HU has been breathed
into us: it is divine consciousness.

a clay animal immediately aware of itself.

metaphors for the taste of pomegranate.

be weary of the marketplace,
where only imaginary things are sold.

i would be impossible and nothing
without the majesty of the divine gallop.
so ride your horse quickly away into the desert…
… . … .. . .

…dropping a trail of dung as you go…

…the flowers will always follow.

φ

and of all that i've ever read or seen,
there lingers only one thing that
remains the image of images for me:
an unknown bird sitting silently
upon my best friend's tomb:
oh the majesty you always become.

φ

where was it, when?
the divine wave dissolved
me into an ocean from a drop.
i wondered in longing for you.
a sad pilgrim, the sought.
you were my feet upon,
as well as, the dirt tickling me
on that not so lonely
damascus road.

do the leaves also think they
are absent of the eternal life,
until the wind comes kissing?

φ

thank you for bidding on my soul
such a long time ago at the auction.
you drove that elephant stark into
the marketplace with a Love-heart
and the drunk-song of birds, perching
their gold feet upon your arms.

i have lain down and become fire
just to praise you in my gratitude.
i was the bedraggled boy,
a lonely splash in your bucket
almost lost to the infinite desert,
but you made me an ocean complete,
right when i thought id evaporate.
and now the moon makes me dance
inside your heart, rising with the tides.

φ

i desire the rope-burned wrists of Love.
please, Friend. tie me, deafen me.
there is only one song i've ever craved.
you make the heart complete.

she comes rising through
the orange sky,
shy & smiling,
my eternal home
and rest,

my moonfaced Penelope: Love.

φ

eyes closed, still.
stars swarming
cosmic circles
overhead.

it was not a mirror.
the unspeakable was.

stare directly.

the swirling universe's
dancing love-soul within:
unanswerable, clairvoyant.

φ

days like this, days like this.
alexandria's library burning.
let it.
the pantheon flooding.
the gods choking on their own love.

pages flutter & fizzle into the air,
returning to their former wind life in trees.

nights like this: coming, inevitable.

i am laughing as the horsemen circle.

put the arrows into my knees.
break me into the final bow.
bring the blade through my neck.
i want to kiss the ground one last time.

this will all pass.
days and nights like this.

i have always been made of rain.
sopping with love-longing
for the space beyond clouds.

φ

more than chess,
the hands of love move me.
everyone peers into illusion.

i remember the blade carving
my true soul shape. it is faint.

it keeps me amazed,
staring at the geometry below.

arrogance moves itself,
direct and into death.

but i, i gallop in love's freedom,
the untethered existence
only attained in surrender.

felt-kissed, soft angel earth.
the sun feels dizzy drunk
from all the attentive twirling.

he closes night eyes,
knowing only moon-lips
can come to you in darkness.

wrap yourself in the night blanket.
let it cut off your breathing.
you do not own it anyways.

let the hand cut down barren
corn stalks and open the path.
we all crave the taste of blood.

topple the false king
and wait, patiently.

who saw those stars
like blooming flowers all along?

who trained the lion
to lick the wounded?

who's baby voice,
laughing in our garden?

the queen has risen.
you are safe now.

ϙ

i am not the radiant gardener.
i did not bring upon this creation.
i do not possess much wisdom.
i am aware of some things.
the lotus in our pond here
needs the dark sludge of mud

to fully grow itself into beauty,
just like the rose has shit thrown on her,
yet produces the scent of heaven and blushes.

starve your berries of a little water,
they will become perfectly sweet;
over water your peppers
and they'll lose their spiciness.
it is not so much what is taken in,
but what it is all turned into, though.

this riddled balance of give and take.
dance your dead skin off like a snake.

sometimes it takes a lot of pruning
to bring the fruit tree back to life.
never mistake the pain of being torn apart
for anything but the greatest love of all!

all that fucking magical majesty
that is marching over mountains
to find you
to fill you!

φ

gracious eyes,
i've chased you,
my hidden shadow.
heart of gratitude,
i've burned in the sun,
my eyes focused on
the mystery of how
your shape was always there.
funny how i trip over myself and fall right into you.

♀

an atom hellbent on singing
its own song amongst a chorus.

a star burning to be known
or simply seen is only
committing suicide.

calm every particle of your holy being.

you are just a particle
of the entire magnificent *beingness*.

quit fighting with such force.
you'll upset your lover's stomach.

instead, become silent peace.

whisper angel lullabies
to every stardust speck
floating the heavenly dark-sky dance
inside the blanket of your flesh.

drop the cloth and shimmer.

you will be a honey salve
that gives a love-soothing
to all that universe beauty.

♀

all love,
given or received,
is commendable.

love is water:
nourisher, infinite.

by no strange coincidence
is it the main ingredient
within the loaf of bread
and also the human dough.

our souls are cosmic diamonds,
made perfect and indestructible.

but our hearts are pliable,
cooked in love's kitchen
with a few precise ingredients:
pain and laughter and love.

we rise from soft nothing
into our higher form,
eager to be consumed
by our lovely bread maker.

suddenly,
we stop being so wounded by the salt,
and we feel the honey mixing within us,
knowing heaven's lips
are closer to us
than ever before.

φ

chrysalis

life is often perceived to be cruel.
even the most beautiful
are seen crawling about
dripping poison from their lips.
the tears make our eyes shut.
but force them back open to see!

the dead are wrapped in gold
and given silent, beautiful wings.

this makes all our art just look stupid.

φ

the human mind
has its scared claws
dug into a single grain of sand.
and im just screaming:
"but look! there's a whole
desert surrounding you,
upon a beautiful planet,
floating in an infinite universe!"
if you do anything heroic
in your entire lifetime,
let it be this:
just once, laugh so fucking hard
that your eyes are filled with tears
and you almost die from lack of oxygen.
why?
because you will smile ear to ear
when you hear the echo
come back to you
in a few million years.

♀

sleepy, absalom!
you pulled the heart's curtain.
closed eyed in a night cave,
i've been blind all my life.
but you kissed my soul awake
with your angel hot breath,
my perfect, golden heavenbird.

now the unseen cannot be unseen!

even when i close my eyes,
my eyelids are universes
swimming in starlight.

♀

no need to kill time.
it's suicide prone
and dying on its own.
throw the clocks away,
or lie them on their backs
and lower them into the earth.
that way they can join in
and do nature's love dance.
get naked and climb a tree.
watch the stars dropping their shields
like flower petals into a giant ocean,
holding hands, spinning,
painting creation on the water's surface,
where you'll find me there making silence.

φ

"Love loves loving you!"
the Friend is singing lullabies again.
but your ears have broken
and your soul is haunted.

the prophet has been stuffing
his mouth full of snow.

pray for death by lightning.
let the flesh peel off easily
like an orange burnt in embers.

become soft and sweet to the lips.
drip forever
from a springtime angel's mouth.

φ

we stole you away, daylight star.
i watched you being planted
under the half-moon's crescent smile.
you were laid down next to
your beet brothers and sage sisters.
"cocooned heart — forever reborn."
we sang circles,
watching Her night womb swell.
"seed split, earth grit, heaven spit:
we're all returning to you!"
the roots grow.
sprouted broccoli bones.
from tomato tombs,
Love leafs come reaching for you!

φ

a bowl of lentils

there is a song within
that makes no sound.
its enchantment is that silence.

there are no distinctions:
east or west, up or down,
only Love in this holy palace.

i was not hungry
but you offered me a bowl of lentils.
a flower floating in the field.
the stars blushing as i fill my mouth.

φ

i spoke with an ant man,
who assured me our world
was smaller than a grain of sand.

as an old woman rode
a turkey into town,
singing "*it's circles, circles
all the way down!*"

the Mystery is smiling
right before your eyes —
but from deep inside.

♀

i memorized mountains
like they were pretty psalms.
i prayed for an index of words
that only you would hear.
your hidden heart,
my timeless talisman.
listless laughter leads us
when all compasses are broken.
the dial dances drunkenly
as our guide when you are near.

celestial caliph! ship-sinker!
polish my somber soul.
i am but a few drops of mildew
upon your domed astrolabe.

my sweet-mouthed star-talker!
dissolve the illusion and me
like wave-crashed foam,
longing to become the sea.

take me back to the place
where creation is not an act or thing,
but another word for Love.

♀

i've receded into the singularity.
my death has become a whisper.
this world is an olive on a tree
that sleeps atop a saint's slope.

ϕ

i've been looking for you everywhere,
blind watchmaker! lovestruck key-carver!
fools' fingers are pointing in every direction.
but the insane know the answer,
the beautiful-majestic-glorious joke!

gather round!
my heart has caught fire.
watch: i've flung my body off the cliff
to split like firewood on the rocks.

i've found the Friend,
buried beyond time
tucked into a crack in the wall
of my given soul.

ϕ

tired old fisherman,
it's been days since
you've eaten anything.
you drop the net
into the night sea again.
pull it out and set it aflame!
cast your invisible infinite net
into the sea of all love.
there are fire jewels
swimming all around you.
close your eyes and see.

ϕ

come now. quickly.
the Beloved One
is moving near.
shadow-eater!
eyes of snow!
mouth of light!
friends...all:
smash your clay bowls
against the cave walls.
dance because you're dying
and you know what it is to live again!

no more measuring!
the bodiless dimension calls you.

hang up the old garments,
wiggle into the soft dirt!

move like Love's water
toward the overflowing fountain,
carving your way home
through hardened stone.

ϕ

let the fear fall like a fig
dropping to the ground.
be not claustrophobic,
crying out in confused pain.

wings are budding like flowers
from your fallen spotted scales.
you crawl in this life,
not the one that follows.

the first tree is the thread.
the second tree is the needle.
the third tree is a lesson.

realize your nakedness.
let the garments fall.
your roots grow straight towards heaven,
your soul is the garden.

rise up, my love,
my fair one, and come away.
the grapes are ripening
underneath the spring bird.

love whispers softly into the wind,
and your ears perk up listening:
the wheat and barley,
the vines and pomegranate,
the pressed olives and honey.

softer, softer now.
the sycamore's secret: a song.

φ

*lovers hang like silkworms
suspended upside down,
weaving impossibilities
that stretch from tree stumps
beyond mountaintops,
swinging from star to star.*

φ

this poison was once an antidote.
this serpent was once a staff.
this scream was once a baby's laugh.

this fruit was once a tiny seed.
this garden was once a barren field.
that flying bird, once an empty egg.
that singing violin, once a cut down tree.

skies blue and cheerful.
breath's heavy heaving.
lightning touches the earth.

sun-dried tears, too much rain.
what once was will surely be again.

the eternal law of shape-shifters:
the dandelion changes her dress and blows away;
a beautiful blossom dies to become
sweet red fruit for you;
the trilobite gets naked for life's final season.

a tree bows humbly with fruit.

i am mimicry in a mockingbird's mouth:
nothing less, nothing more.

lowered down and risen up,
the hymn and the harp.